Ah, Wisconsin!

Ah, Wisconsin!

A photographic revelation by RICHARD HAMILTON SMITH

With a dozen lively tales from HOWARD MEAD

WISCONSIN TRAILS   *Madison, Wisconsin*

For all people who love Wisconsin.

Published by Wisconsin Trails Magazine,
a division of Wisconsin Tales and Trails, Inc.,,
P.O. Box 5650, Madison, Wisconsin 53705

Copyright © 1990 Wisconsin Trails Magazine
Photographs copyright © 1990 Richard Hamilton Smith
Text copyright © 1990 Howard Mead
Library of Congress Catalog Card Number 90-70601
International Standard Book Number 0-915024-35-7

Design: Paul Fuchs Design, Madison
Color Separations: Color 4 Graphics, Inc., Milwaukee
Printing: Universal Lithographers Incorporated, Sheboygan

"Ah, Wisconsin!" is printed on 110# Eloquence
text-weight paper from Potlatch Corporation,
an acid-free paper of the highest quality.

Printed in the United States of America
First Printing: July, 1990

Chiwaukee Prairie.

In celebration of the beauty of Wisconsin, with special appreciation to the Wisconsin Chapter of The Nature Conservancy for its work in preserving the wonderful diversity of our natural world.

Contents

Ah, Wisconsin. For all the people who have been inspired to utter these words, here is cause to repeat them again and again.

Ah, Wisconsin! Part discovery, part reflection, part celebration, this

INTRODUCTION

*Richard
Hamilton
Smith
and
Howard
Mead*

book merges two remarkable personal visions into a fascinating journey through Wisconsin. Through the photographic images of master photographer Richard Hamilton Smith, we are taken on a breathtaking visual odyssey. Reading the evocative essays of lifelong storyteller Howard Mead, we return to the scenes of our own Wisconsin experiences. From the delicate blend of their artistry–the stunning visual images and the vital, resonant prose–emerges a captivating harmony.

There is magic on every page of *Ah, Wisconsin!* Richard Hamilton Smith's photography startles and inspires the viewer. A Wisconsin scene you thought you knew so well is suddenly revealed in an astonishingly new light. By focusing on only a portion of a larger scene, isolating patterns of light, color and shadow, skillfully manipulating the expanded view of a wide-angle lens or the compression of the telephoto, this artist/photographer presents new perspectives on themes we all know and love in Wisconsin.

It has been said that poets spend their entire lives running around in thunderstorms hoping to be struck by lightning. That same could be said of Richard Hamilton Smith, except in his case, the metaphor carries a literal interpretation. Lightning might be crackling all around him, but he'll totally ignore it until he's got his shot, or better yet, make it the focus of the shot. He thinks nothing of hanging out of a two-seater plane to capture that perfect aerial. He has stood shivering thigh-deep in the muck of a northern marsh to freeze a single fleeting moment.

The dozen stories by Howard Mead bring a down-to-earth quality of shared experiences to *Ah, Wisconsin!* You feel like you're talking to an old friend, sharing a canoe with him, or a ski trail, or a campfire. You understand where he's coming from because you've been there too. And if you haven't, you'll soon be feeling like you have.

Howard Mead is by turns wry, funny, thoughtful, whimsical, a story-teller who has had many laughs on himself. He has a keen, observant eye and an ear tuned to the rhythms of the land. His perceptions and an easy candor wrap each of his tales around some small, precious truth that relates to all of our lives.

For thirty years, Howard and his wife Nancy have been publishing *Wisconsin Trails* magazine. Together they've covered a lot of territory in those years, growing to know and love this place like few of us ever have the chance to. These stories share the best of those experiences.

Richard Hamilton Smith and Howard Mead traveled separate roads in their discoveries of the treasures of Wisconsin. From the record of their journeys has emerged a book of rare vision, full of the immense beauty of this state and steeped in the great joys of life here. *Ah, Wisconsin!*

Rock Island's western shoreline, Door County.

Pasqueflower at Thousand's Rock Point Prairies, Dane County.

Ferns touched with frost, Seeley.

Autumn on One Man Lake, Mercer.

A big muskie is an awesome sight–a powerful, vicious-looking
fish with a cruel, undershot jaw, a mouthful of razor teeth, and
malevolent, amber eyes set high in a narrow skull. It's not an image

M U S K I E S

that's easily forgotten. Especially by a thirteen-year-old boy.
It was on the famed Chippewa Flowage, over forty years ago,
that my grandfather and I had an encounter with a monster
muskellunge, which since has become a family legend. My
grandfather loved to fish, especially for walleyes and bass. And
although he was a skilled angler, superb with a fly rod, fishing for
muskie was another game entirely.

To learn this new game, we had signed on for an entire week of
muskie fishing with a silver-tongued resort owner we met at a sports
show. "Your grandson will love it," he had said. "Catching one of
those brutes will be an experience he'll never forget." I'm sure,
based on his glowing description, that I expected to catch a muskie
or two each day. He never mentioned "throw and retrieve." Or told
us about the heavy artificial baits with tiny propellers at each end.
Throw and retrieve. How do you describe monotony? A backlash
was excitement. Tremendous excitement was motoring to a new
spot. Some say it takes 10,000 casts to catch a muskie. These are
the optimists.

The days dragged by, hot, sticky, the sun's blinding rays ricochet-
ing like bullets off the water. The guide looked and talked just about
the way I thought a guide should. Rumpled, grizzled, cheek filled
with Mail Pouch chewing tobacco, he rowed the boat deftly and told
outrageous stories. After the first day's throwing and retrieving, my
grandfather took the guide aside and told him, on account of the
boy, to clean up his language and to please spit downwind whenever
possible. It was a very long week.

"Howard," my grandfather said on the last evening, "I've never been so glad to come to the end of a fishing trip. I can't lift an arm to throw another plug. But if you want to have one last try, I can probably muster the strength to row a short way for you."

I had taken only a couple of casts when the water around my lure erupted. "Set the hook," shouted Grandfather, who never shouted. I whaled away at this unseen, powerful force that threatened to pull me out of the boat. The muskie leaped once, exploding straight up out of the water, shaking its head trying to free the bait. It was a very big fish.

"Heaven help us," said Grandfather.

Dusk became darkness and the battle raged on. Details? Who can remember. Grandfather at the oars, indistinct in the night, except for his pale yellow straw hat. The resort was only a small circle of light a couple of hundred yards down the lake and slowly he rowed us toward it. "Do you need help?" came a shout. "No, we're all right. We have a fish on," called Grandfather.

As we neared the beach, the fish was still lunging powerfully against my noodle arms. We didn't have a net so we were going to have to beach it. When the light seemed right above us, a knot of excited people beneath it, Grandfather, who must have thought we were as good as on shore, stepped out to guide the boat in and grab the fish. Unfortunately, the water was still deep. There was a loud splash. All I could see over my shoulder, as I strained against the huge fish, was his hat drifting away into the darkness. Then he bobbed up, spluttering, his white hair plastered down on his head. More shouts. Helping hands. And then we were on the beach, wet, slimy, sandy and tangled in the line–the muskie clutched between us. There are those moments in life you never forget. And for me this was one of them–the sight of my grandfather, a reserved, soft-spoken, gentlemanly man beside me in the sand, the head of that fifty-two-inch monster cradled in his lap.

Cutting a foggy course down the Mississippi, Grant County.

Early morning departure, Danbury.

Anglewing butterfly at Rush Creek Bluffs, Crawford County.

Bloodroot in early spring sunlight, Trempealeau.

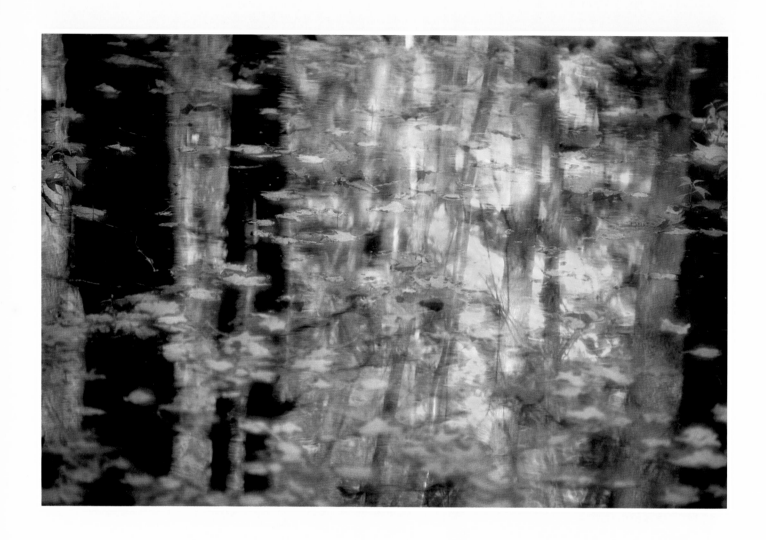

Autumn mirrored in Crab Lake, Presque Isle.

Reflection of the State Capitol, Madison.

Our "farm," tucked among the steep-sided hills of Iowa County, is a magical place of quiet beauty. But when I think of the times we had there as a family, weekends and summers and spontaneous

ERNIE AND ALBERT

overnights, I don't remember so much the solitude and haunting wildness as I do our outrageous country neighbors, the Peterson brothers, who for many years were as much a part of going to the farm as the farm itself.

The first weekend we ever spent there was the worst weekend I ever spent anywhere. It rained buckets. We simply tried to survive in a tiny tent pitched alongside the old log cabin–two adults and three children, one of them a month old. The cabin's roof was caving in, its interior smelled like a zoo and when we banged on the keys of the old upright piano, three flying squirrels scurried out the back.

Into our "paradise" came Ernie and Albert Peterson on a little, gray Ford tractor–Albert driving and Ernie balancing on the back. They had come to check on the new city folks, to offer a neighborly welcome. Ernie was the talker, bluff and cheerful. Albert was small, wizened and quiet. Usually he squatted with his back against a tree or wall, on the edge of things, just listening and watching and smoking menthol cigarettes right down to the filter. It was Ernie who expounded enthusiastically with an inexhaustible supply of country wisdom.

"What did you buy the cabin for?" he asked, looking at our bedraggled tent. "Aren't you going to use it?"

I waved toward the collapsing roof and told him I'd hired a carpenter to replace it. "You don't need to do that," said Ernie. "We'll come over and give you a hand." I was warmed by this display of neighborliness, but I told him I'd already made the deal.

As they got up to leave, Ernie pointed to the ramshackle, tarpaper shed that had been patched onto the front of the cabin. "Seen the woodchuck?" he asked. "He's real big," added Albert. So far we'd only seen the large hole in the floor of the lean-to.

"We'll give you a hand digging him out," Ernie offered, as Albert started the tractor. A couple of weeks later I discovered what "we'll give you a hand" meant. It meant I would spend a couple of hours digging while the Peterson brothers smoked, drank coffee, ate brownies, talked with Nancy, and complimented me on how handy I was with a shovel. The woodchuck must have been visiting neighbors because we never got "down" to him. When I'd made a hole the size of a bomb crater, Ernie announced that it was time to do the milking. "Better put a board across that pit," he suggested, "so the little kids won't fall in."

It was a game. The Peterson brothers loved to watch other people work. I came to the country for relaxation. But Ernie and Albert had other ideas. We were their weekend entertainment. Time after time they'd "help" get a project started–propping up a tilting corncrib, digging a drainage ditch so the barn wouldn't wash out, or best of all, tearing down a building that was beyond salvation. At the exact moment the immensity of the project overtook me, they'd announce it was time to visit another neighbor or "time to do the milking."

To the Petersons we were curiosities. Why would anyone pay good money for one hundred and twenty acres of useless, red clay hillsides and sandstone outcrops? Or spend hours clearing and mowing an elaborate system of trails, up hill and down, through blackberries and underbrush? To ski on? So the small children wouldn't get lost? And the log sauna we built? "You mean you just sit there and bake? And then you jump in a horse trough full of cold water?" asked Ernie. "Why?" added Albert.

Over the years they taught us country ways. Ernie captured a swarm of bees in a bushel basket and we became beekeepers. We helped shear sheep, searched the woods for missing heifers, hefted hay bales, used the kids' swift young legs to run down countless ducks, geese and roosters, made crocks of wild grape wine and took long circuitous jaunts to find the best blackberry patches. No weekend ever ended without a visit to the Petersons' to buy eggs, help with the milking, and catch up with the local gossip.

The Peterson brothers are gone now and our children grown and moved away. What little time I spend at the farm these days is usually spent alone, keeping things tidy and roaming through the hills, as wild and as lovely as when we first saw them so many years ago. The other day, poking around in the basement, I found a bottle of wild grape wine that Ernie Peterson had given me. For a moment I thought of taking it along on my next trip to the farm; of opening it there and drinking a toast to all those wonderful memories. But then I remembered how Ernie's wine tasted, and I put the bottle back. The memories could stand very nicely on their own.

Squirrel on a corncrib, Eastman.

Barn painting near Brussels.

Patchwork fields, Glenwood City.

Hanging the tobacco harvest, Cambridge.

Late snowfall, Nelson.

Cows on the Concourse, Madison.

Barn art near Delavan.

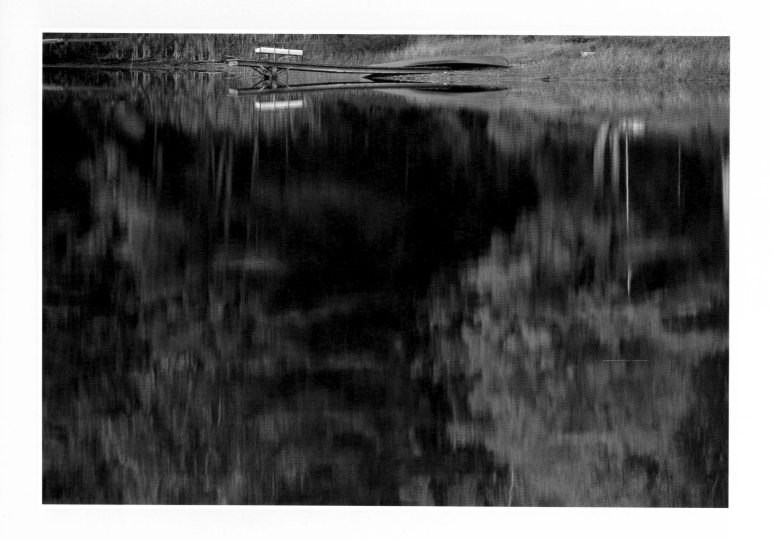

Canoe at rest on Loon Lake, Ashland County.

At anchor on peaceful Lake Michigan, Marinette.

The biggest thing that ever happened to Wisconsin was the glacier, last seen heading north out of the state one hundred centuries ago. This prodigious giant stood a mile or more tall and covered millions

G L A C I E R

of square miles. And as it disappeared, it gave the Wisconsin landscape its final shape, created our sparkling lakes and rearranged our rivers.

Picture an immense snowdrift, thousands of feet deep, a mindboggling accumulation of countless centuries, so massive it covered half the continent. Imagine the enormous weight compressing the snow into ice, squeezing downward, forcing gigantic tongues outward in every direction, ponderously scraping and gouging, bulldozing off hills, digesting rocks, filling valleys, detouring rivers, leveling forests.

Then it all changed. Centuries of milder weather gnawed away at the glacier. It melted gradually, moving by fits and starts, falling back then grinding forward again, icy water pouring like sweat off its rounded brow. Inside, the glacier was a great churning cement mixer, engulfing and pulverizing rocks of every size, which, as the ice melted, were unloaded in great quantities as rich soils in one place and fine sand or rocks in another. The glacier advanced, pulled by gravity, flowing outward from its area of greatest thickness near Hudson Bay, scraping and screeching across bedrock. But it melted back quietly, a vast ice field, turning to slush, wasting away.

This last glacier left behind Wisconsin's varied landscape like no other. How could we be so lucky? What an incredible diversity of shape and form is Wisconsin! Drumlins shaped like fat cigars halfburied; eskers, sinuous humpbacked ridges; kames that look like gumdrops; and deep kettles, pitting the countryside. Everywhere across Wisconsin are gifts of the glacier—our abundant lakes as well as the tilt and shape of the land; the north country's boulder-strewn, rolling ridges perfect for growing magnificent forests; our bogs and marshes and bubbling springs; Lake Michigan and Lake Superior, our inland seas, gouged out to depths of one thousand feet; and our fertile farmlands.

Twenty times during the Ice Age great glaciers lumbered across Wisconsin. Each time they surrounded, bypassed and left untouched the rugged hill and valley country of the Driftless Area, our stunningly beautiful southwest corner, unique in all the world. This Denmark-sized chunk of Wisconsin looks the same as it did before the Ice Age began two million years ago–a lakeless land of crags and pinnacles, caves and natural bridges.

And up north. Just look at all the blue specks and squiggles on the map of Wisconsin. Every one is a lake or river. The Ojibwa called Wisconsin "a gathering of the waters." What an incredible bounty of water we have–nearly 15,000 lakes and a million acres of water surface. In Vilas and Oneida counties there are probably more natural lakes clustered together than anywhere else in the world–nearly a thousand in the two counties combined. And these are only the lakes with names. There are nearly an equal number with no names at all.

Why don't we recognize the glacier's matchless gifts to Wisconsin? Why don't we celebrate? We hold a thousand festivals or more in our state every year. Why not one to acclaim Wisconsin's most extraordinary event? A special day every summer when each Wisconsinite and visitor would travel to their favorite lake or river to celebrate the glacier's gift. You might water-ski on it, squirting a watery rooster tail of silvery fragments as you go. You might paddle your canoe down a wild and beautiful river, or run your sailboat with the wind, spinnaker flying. You could surround your boat with a lake and fish, or simply sit beside it, swathed in the rosy glow of a summer sunset. Ah, Wisconsin. A gathering of the waters. Thanks to the glacier.

Maple leaves adrift on the Petenwell Flowage, Adams County.

Frosty morning on the Wisconsin River, Plover.

Spring violets at Hoffman Hills, Colfax.

An early spring snow, Nelson.

Gull tracks in the sand of Stockton Island.

Riding out the dawn near Holy Hill, Hubertus.

Swept up in the Tidal Wave, Wisconsin Dells.

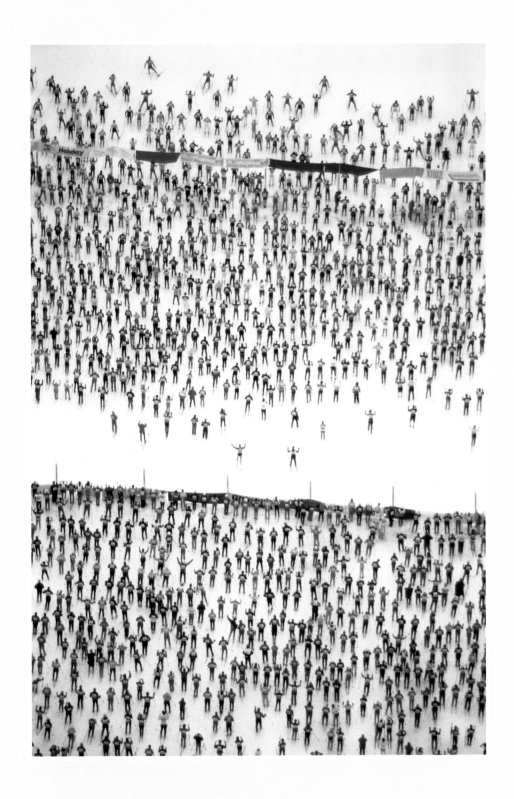

Skiers at the American Birkebeiner, Hayward.

What can you do with that little, woefully inadequate sliver of the Wisconsin year from late March to early April? I can offer only two bits of advice: go fly a kite or visit a sugar bush!

SUGAR BUSH

For centuries before white men came to Wisconsin, the Indians went to their sugar camps during this time to celebrate the maple moon, the end of the hard, hungry winter and the return to warmer weather. "Sugar making," wrote Indian agent Henry Schoolcraft one hundred and fifty years ago, "was a sort of an Indian carnival." Just what our family needed, we decided. And so for years we acclaimed spring's imminent arrival and turned this nondescript, mini-season into a time of joy and excitement by operating a tiny sugar bush right outside our back door.

The syrup we made was extravagantly delicious and the fun we had making it included the entire neighborhood. A string of kids tramped through the snow lugging brace and bit, spiles and buckets to tap our twelve maples. Everyone had a chance at every job: cranking the drill bit through bark and into the pale wood oozing with sap; tapping the spiles gently in and watching fascinated as the sap began to dribble down. Of course everyone tasted the droplets of the faintly sweet sap, catching them deftly on the tip of their tongues. With great ceremony our buckets, some with peaked lids, others with flaps for covers, were hung. One tree was festooned with two- and three-pound coffee cans suspended from hand-carved sumac spiles, cherished relics from our early years before we acquired "professional" equipment.

Maple syrup begins one drop at a time–every plink against the bottom of the bucket adding to the total. When conditions for the sap run are perfect–freezing nights and bright, clear days with temperatures rising into the forties–the sugar bush is lively with the rapid sound of drops falling, a drumroll for the new season. The precious sap is emptied into big collecting pails and carried, sloshing, through the melting snow and mud to the fire blazing in the rusted cast-iron firebox. At the peak of the sap run, we boil from morning until late at night, continually adding fresh sap to the flat, shallow pans.

The first run of sap is the sweetest–as few as twenty-five gallons of sap boil down to make a gallon of finished syrup. Later in the season it might take sixty. Slowly the sap's water content is evaporated and what remains turns darker and sweeter until, as it nears syrup, the bubbles become smaller and the boiling frantic. With scary suddenness the pans must come off the fire or, in an instant, you have a pan of burnt, caramelized sugar.

Passersby, drawn by the fragrance of wood smoke and the sight of great clouds of vapor rising, joined the group clustered around the boiling pans to watch the thickening sap seethe and froth over the hot fire. "What's going on?" they'd ask. "Just making maple syrup," someone, usually a kid with just a hint of pride, would answer. "You're fooling. Right here in Madison?" Soon they were no longer passing by. They were stoking the fire, adding new sap to the boiling pans, splitting a little oak, or walking down to the maples to see how fast the buckets were filling–beginning to smell well-smoked like the rest of us. And no one ever left for home without a taste of fresh syrup, usually topping a scoop of vanilla ice cream.

The year our youngest daughter Becky went to college she wrote encouraging us to continue the sugar bush. "Remember boots and sloshing around in mud and snow. Pants drenched from too much sap in the bucket. A trail of kids, all wanting to help. Suntanning, watching the fire and breathing nothing but maple-flavored air. Sitting there on a spring night watching the sparks fly toward the stars (the best time for thinking and dreaming). Sticky wallpaper from boiling the syrup to its final perfection inside. The thrill of finally being the kid with all the answers and know-how, after the other two have lost interest. Mud, smoke, wet sugary clothes. What great fun!"

Of course, I remember. How could I ever forget those years when we found the perfect use for Wisconsin's least perfect moment.

Silhouette against nightfall, Platteville.

Bright maples in the Chequamegon National Forest, Ashland County.

Amish boys near Ontario.

Regenerating hemlock in the Mink River Estuary, Rowleys Bay.

A farmer and his horses, Eagle River.

Steam engines at the Rock River Thresheree, Janesville.

Hoarfrost on the landscape, Elk Mound.

Farmhouse on a wintry morning, Fort Atkinson.

Winding country road, Gills Rock.

Lighthouse near Sheboygan on Lake Michigan's icy shore.

I've danced the polka with Poles, taken saunas with Finns, eaten Cornish pasties and Danish aebleskivers, even danced Scottish country dances at my son's wedding. A Swiss friend from New Glarus

LUTEFISK

tried to teach me to yodel, and the Welsh invited me to attend one of their glorious hymn-singing Gymanfa Ganus, provided I just listen. Over the years I have attended festivals galore. I've eaten, danced and sung my way across Wisconsin celebrating our state's wonderful ethnic diversity.

However, I had never, until last fall, eaten lutefisk with the Norwegians. I'd come close, but there are so many rumors about the smell and taste of lutefisk, that frankly, I'd never had the courage to face it. Lutefisk begins as cod that has been dried in the summer sun. As the lutefisk season approaches, the cod is reconstituted in a bath of water charged with lye (yes, lye). Thus softened, the lutefisk is cooked in salty water and served. Great lutefisk is supposed to come out of this tortured preparation "flaky," which I take to mean thin, crisp fragments. "Flaky" must be very difficult to achieve because most descriptions of lutefisk include adjectives like oozy and slimy. These are not words that one associates with great cuisine. They aren't even words that suggest edibility.

I knew there was a lutefisk dinner in my future long before it happened. Every year in November and December, when the lutefisk season swung into high gear, I could feel restless stirrings in my home. Finally, one night last year, Nancy said, "Let's round off the total Wisconsin experience and try the lutefisk this year." That's when I knew I'd better start looking for help. Lutefisk calls forth strong emotions. Most Norwegians and some Swedes love it. Those who don't love it, detest it. Actually there's a third group, those who have married Norwegians and learned to cope with an annual dose of lutefisk for the sake of their marriages.

It was to this last group I turned for advice on how to prepare for what had become an inevitable lutefisk dinner. Their ingenuity was astonishing. "Slip a bottle of Tabasco in your pocket," was one suggestion. "Use mustard," was another. "Cook up a small batch in August and eat a tidbit every day. When the lutefisk season rolls around in November, your immune system will be ready." A friend who had married a Swede advised: "There's more to a lutefisk dinner than lutefisk. Go for the meatballs; they are always great!" My research uncovered a little pamphlet: "Things You've Always Wanted To Know About Lutefisk But Were Too Polite To Ask!" That and a poem called "A Scandahovians Lutefisk Lament" didn't help. They only confirmed my worst fears.

Still, the decision to go was made and a date was chosen. But when we arrived at the Lutheran church, we were confronted by a hand-lettered sign on the door: SORRY ALL OUT OF LUTEFISK. My spirits soared. "Well," I said to Nancy, trying to sound crushed, "looks like we're out of luck." "We'll see," she said, marching determinedly past the sign.

It was a festive scene that greeted us inside. The sound of hundreds of happy voices filled the banquet hall. Smiling women in red caps carried great trays of food. Shirt-sleeved men cleared tables and poured coffee. We were seated with four veteran lutefisk dinner-goers, all very friendly and talkative. Realizing we were first-timers, they solicitously passed the delicious meatballs, coleslaw, cranberry and lingonberry sauces, mashed potatoes, rice pudding and all the other delicacies that made up the feast. They demonstrated buttering and rolling up sugar or cranberry sauce in thin, tasty potato pancakes called lefse.

We were having a very nice time, when "it" appeared. White, almost translucent, in a great steaming bowl, the lutefisk seemed to quiver with a life of its own. But weren't they out? Yes, but Nancy had gone directly to the head cook and discovered a little had been held in reserve. "Your wife didn't want you to be disappointed," said a kind lady as she set the bowl on the table. I took a small, tentative bite. It had the consistency of warm jello with a taste and odor I cannot describe. Perhaps no one can. I tried another bite. Melted butter helped and so did packing it between layers of potatoes. But the real answer lay in rapid palate cleansing–a small bite of lutefisk followed quickly by bites of cranberry, coleslaw and a swallow of coffee. Momentum, I thought, keep at it, one bite following another until it was gone. One of the women at our table smiled and told us that when her mother cooked turkey and lutefisk at the same time, you couldn't smell the turkey. A member of the club now, I could laugh, though weakly.

Each year people drive hundreds of miles following a lutefisk circuit, attending a different dinner every weekend. Why, I wondered? Is this an annual act of affirmation? The indomitable Norwegians against the lutefisk? I glanced around the room at all those people, laughing, talking, eating, thoroughly enjoying themselves in celebration of their heritage. And I looked down at the lutefisk. Not bad, I decided. Not bad at all.

Flocking gulls, Gills Rock.

Fish for the smokehouse, Gills Rock.

Fishing buoys and boathouse in Bayfield.

Misty evening, New Glarus.

Dark reflections on Spirit Lake, Three Lakes.

Farms wrapped in mist, Monroe.

Restored Cornish cottages at Pendarvis, Mineral Point.

Within the Chequamegon National Forest, Grand View.

Island shadows on the Chippewa Flowage, Sawyer County.

I'm always startled when I hear someone complain about the rigors of a Wisconsin winter. But I seldom take them seriously because every year I see the ski hills and trails, the ice rinks and

SPRING HERO

lakes crowded with people having fun. It makes sense. Many of us are, after all, descended from very hardy stock–Germans, Finns, Swedes, Norwegians, Poles, Scots–to name just a few. And if, over time, our blood has thinned a bit, at least we have all learned how to behave in cold weather. Cold, we feel, is exhilarating and energizing. And the prospect of a six-inch snowfall warms our hearts because it is beautiful and because its presence, a blanket covering the land, holds the promise of renewal in spring.

Although a Wisconsin winter is one of life's sublime experiences, it is not considered heresy to glance about occasionally for a hint of spring. At first, as we turn the corner in January, emerging from darkness, the signs of spring are subtle. Just little things. The cardinal, a bright red flash against snow, rediscovers his clear whistle. One late winter morning the chickadee stops saying its name and sings a new two-note spring song in a minor key. And each passing day adds a fraction more light. It is this that we really long for, not for less cold or snow, but for the increasing daylight that sets off the chronology of spring events as certain as the stars.

There are many signs: the welcome clamor of geese returning in wavering lines; rivers and streams filled to the brim by the first real thaw; the rousing chorus of tiny spring peepers, who, for a brief time compose the loudest sound in nature. Some would add the groundhog to this roster of the portents of spring. I, however, maintain February 2 is really a day of fun and folklore. A moment of mid-winter comic relief. How can we take seriously the prognostication of a lumpy rodent who must be revived from a deep hibernation stupor and pushed grumpily from its den in search of its shadow.

But there is, I discovered several years ago, a true Wisconsin folk hero who indicates long before any other creature that spring is indeed waiting in the wings, even in deepest winter. It was a January evening, and Nancy and I were skiing through the darkness, the glow of our miner's headlamps penetrating the night just far enough for us to see the track. The skiing was excellent, the pace exhilarating, until, as we cut through a cluster of oaks, fierce piercing shrieks rang out from the trees directly overhead. Sudden, unearthly sounds told us emphatically to get the heck out of there. And we did, fast, the lunatic screams chasing us through the blackness. Once in the car with the motor running, our heartbeats returning to normal, we speculated that since cougars were not a possibility it had to be owls. Indeed, we learned later it was–great horned owls in the midst of their mating ritual.

Another year we discovered a great horned owl nesting in a tall cottonwood just west of our home. On a sub-zero day in February, standing well back from the tree, we could just see the female's head with its distinctive tufts above the snow-covered edge of the nest. There she was, sitting on her eggs in the worst weather of the year, pelted by sleet, buffeted by cold winds. And there she would gallantly remain for a month while her mate, on wings as silent as smoke, hunted for them both. We went back often to watch the enormous-eyed young owlets, all beaks and claws, clad in thick suits of down that looked like fuzzy long johns. For another ten weeks their parents flew a food-shuttle service to satisfy their bottomless appetites. When spring finally arrived in April, with a rush and a clamor, bringing an abundance of food, the young owls were ready to fend for themselves.

Now, as we glide through January and February nights, our excursions have an added dimension–to listen for the earliest sign of spring we know, the eerie, resonating call of great horned owls echoing through the winter woods. If the owls are nesting, spring must be stirring, even in February.

Apple orchard in bloom, Chippewa Falls.

Apple orchard in winter, Chippewa Falls.

Witchgrass in the Gasser Sand Barrens, Sauk City.

Anemone and ginger, Browntown.

Opening salute at the World Lumberjack Championships, Hayward.

Male wild turkey, Galesville.

The Great Circus Parade, Milwaukee.

Preparing for flight, Wisconsin Dells.

On the map, Rock Island is a remote chip of land off the tip of Door County, out beyond Washington Island. Heavily forested, bordered by towering limestone cliffs rising from Lake Michigan

R O C K I S L A N D

on the north and west and a sweeping sand beach along the south shore, Rock Island is Wisconsin's most remote state park–a place of peace and solitude.

Once, from the long crescent of beach, Nancy and I and our children watched a towering thunderhead drift toward us, a sinister cauliflower cloud rumbling deep inside. More clouds blossomed, swelling like giant hot air balloons, and flashes of lightning darted back and forth between them. When the sound of thunder was one continuous roar, we dashed for our tent tucked behind the sand dune above the beach. And just in time. The storm ripped open with a blinding flash and a jarring crack. In a house, we scarcely would have noticed. Alone on Rock Island, separated from the storm's fury by only thin fabric, we felt very involved. But the onslaught was brief and as the sound of thunder retreated, we emerged to watch the storm's black and purple back move across the lake trailing softly falling rain.

I have always felt a potent sense of isolation on this island, of being unprotected and close to the natural world. If a gale blows up, you can't climb into your car and drive to a motel. You are stranded, no longer in control. Here, time is suspended. Schedules are switched off, the pace slowed and slowed again.

All the familiar noises–traffic and telephones and radios–abruptly vanish. In their place come elemental sounds–the rhythm of waves brushing across the sand, or of heavy surf pounding against the limestone ledges. Overhead the cry of herring gulls and along sun-dappled woodland trails the dreamy whistle of a white-throated sparrow.

It is a good day's work to explore the island's perimeter, combing the rocky cobble beaches, watching for the shadows of great fish moving through the clear water and wondering about the ocean-going freighters steaming down the lake. After supper, sometimes, we'd walk around the point of land that separates the wild side of Rock Island from remnants of Chester Thordarson's baronial estate. Sitting on the concrete dock alongside his huge stone boathouse and "Icelandic" great hall, watching the sun slip silently out of sight, we'd wonder about the man who built this incongruous monument. This genius inventor and iron-willed millionaire tried to tame this wild island and build his romantic notion of an Icelandic village. Today, most of what he built is gone, but the deer, the "nuisances" he tried to "exterminate" because they ate his exotic plantings, are still here.

The nights are magic, lying on the warm sand stargazing, the Milky Way a brilliant arc spanning the entire sky. We awoke one morning after such a night, in a vaporous soup. Cut off entirely from the rest of the world, we paced the beach, not wanting to venture into the woods, even on a well-marked trail, in fog so thick. As we walked, I told the children tales of all the travelers who, through time beyond memory, had pulled their fragile bark canoes up on this beach, built their fires and waited out the great storms, or waited, like us, for the fog to lift. Of Indians who had camped here summers to fish with spear and hook and line. And of explorers who passed this way searching for the Northwest Passage that they hoped would lead them to the riches of the Orient. Of black-robed missionaries and of the tough little French-Canadian voyageurs, able to portage immense loads and paddle tremendous distances, singing as they went.

We walked along the same beach, camped close to where they had camped. And it seemed as though nothing had changed. A mystical moment, the fog gray and dense, dampening all sound except the swish of the waves on the sand, a sound so similar to canoe paddle strokes that I felt an urge to shout, "Bonjour, Messieurs" into the mysterious murk. And so, half expecting an answer, I did.

Daybreak at Cana Island Lighthouse, Baileys Harbor.

Wildcat Mountain view over Ontario.

Quiet morning at historic Stonefield Village, Cassville.

A view to Lake Michigan, Milwaukee.

Farm reflection, Richland County.

A harvest of cranberries, Tomah.

Autumn view over the Chippewa Flowage, Sawyer County.

Pumpkins on display, Madison.

Every August, when that first confused maple startles us by turning red, I've wished for the gift of prophecy so I might predict when and where Wisconsin's autumn colors will reach their peak of perfection.

AUTUMN RIVER

I have such great expectations. In my mind's eye, I am surrounded by the glory of gleaming orange maples, and birches as well, their leaves burnished copper, each leaf perfectly in place as though styled by a master coiffeur. It would be an epic day, touched with a cool freshness, the sky intensely blue, the trees vivid, and the sunlight soft and diffuse, giving the sensation of being included in an impressionist painting.

My dream is perfect. But always, it seems, when I arrive hoping to experience the prime of autumn, most of the leaves lay scattered on the ground and those that remain on the trees are past their prime, bedraggled and faded. I've come within a hairsbreadth and found leaves so newly fallen they still gleam like bright jewels in the grass. And occasionally I am taunted by a glimpse of a single, impeccable tree. Close, ever so close, but mostly it is: "You should have been here last week."

Still I assure you that a quintessential autumn day is out there waiting to be discovered. Several years ago, I had a tantalizing encounter with such a day–a flawless synchronization of light and color. A day that you might search a lifetime for. But as it turned out, it was not quite what I had expected.

It was early morning of the first Saturday in October when we plunked our canoes into the Wolf River at Hollister to paddle down to Langlade. The little rock garden rapids there sparkled in sunlight. A touch of frost rimmed the spears of grass with silver. And on both sides of the river, the trees seemed to vibrate with colors of such magnitude that I found myself fumbling for my sunglasses.

At flood the Wolf is a river to be reckoned with. But on this day, on this stretch, it was welcoming. The Wolf, at any water level, is beautiful and wild–noisy in the rapids, sometimes sleek and swift and invariably flowing with a discernible downhill pitch. We felt the lively river through the bottom of the canoe, throbbing against the soles of our shoes. In a mountain ash, elegant black-masked cedar waxwings flitted among orange berries. Mallards flushed noisily ahead. And when the current swept the canoe close to shore, an earthy, musty smell mingled with the fragrance of cedar. The river moved us on, as we basked in the incredible beauty of the morning, paddling downstream, dodging rocks, running small rapids.

You will then understand that it came as a terrible shock when this amiable day began to cloud over. The all-blue sky became occasional blue patches among dark clouds. And then there was no blue at all. Heavy and gray, the sky drooped. Big drops of rain began to bang on the canoes with the slow cadence of a funeral march. As the day became increasingly bleak, the rain ceased, replaced by a persistent, chilling mist. Feathery ribbons of fog rose and hung suspended over the river. Leaves fell like ghostly waterfalls to float beside us. In the subdued light, the reds and oranges and yellows of maple, birch and aspen glowed iridescent against the dark green background of conifers. It was ethereal, unforgettable. But from where we were, in the middle of fog rising and mist falling, it was miserable as well. Paddling downriver surrounded by the most opulent display of color we had ever seen, all we could think of was getting to the car and dry clothes and hot coffee.

Every paddle stroke of that trip is indelibly imprinted in my memory–the astonishing beauty we were passing, and the wet and cold too. But you know, the way the mind works is quite wonderful. For now, years later, when I reflect on that trip down the Wolf, I find I can easily eliminate the rain and make the sun shine all day–autumn perfection just the way I had always dreamed it. But then that wouldn't be Wisconsin would it? Better, I think, to recall that rare day just as it happened.

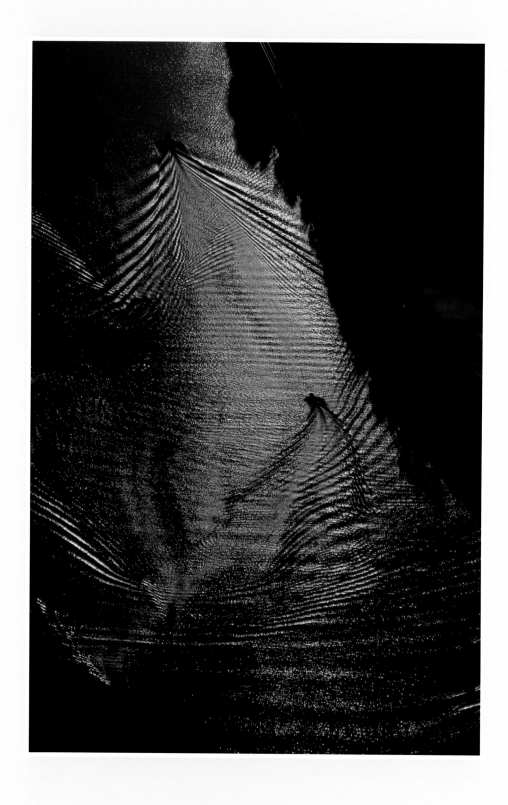

Skimming the Mississippi, Prescott.

Rolling hills of autumn color, Menomonie.

Fallen leaves at Villa Louis, Prairie du Chien.

A golden moment on the Interstate, Tomah.

UW Marching Band practice, Madison.

Ripe cranberries flooded for harvesting, Tomah.

Copper Falls State Park, Mellen.

Snow along the St. Croix River at Dairyland.

It's not every day one has a chance to meet royalty in Wisconsin. But I did one sunlit afternoon in May of 1976. It was at a place I consider to be one of our state's treasures–the outdoor ethnic museum Old

THE QUEEN

World Wisconsin, just then being built in the rumpled hills and dips of the Southern Kettle Moraine near Eagle.

On that lovely day, in the year of our nation's two hundredth birthday, a crowd of several thousand waited eagerly for the arrival of Her Majesty Queen Margrethe II of Denmark. The occasion of the queen's coming was to dedicate a humble log house, the newest addition to the museum, built by a Danish immigrant over a century before. A gentle breeze stirred the flags and banners. Secret Service men, their mirror sunglasses flashing, moved restlessly around the covered dais. As president of the State Historical Society of Wisconsin and the day's master of ceremonies I, too, was pacing, muttering to myself, still memorizing my sheaf of instructions on proper conduct and decorum.

At precisely four o'clock Queen Margrethe, Prince Henrik and the royal party in a caravan of limousines swept to a stop between the speaker's platform and the house. Queens run on tight schedules and strict protocol. The dedication ceremony, planned to the minute, proceeded at a fast clip–the flags were presented, national anthems sung, a group of young people danced, and Girl Scouts brought gifts to the queen. Introductions were made with dispatch and the speeches that followed were short. Through it all the queen, a very tall, handsome woman upon whom all eyes were focused, remained a silent, regal presence.

After she snipped the red ribbon, Queen Margrethe led the official party into the house that the Danish immigrant Kristen Pedersen had built. I found myself beside her peeking into the tiny kitchen. Our eyes met. How does one address a queen? My elaborate guidelines hadn't covered this possibility. Actually the implication was that there simply would not be an opportunity to converse with the queen. Still, one can't stand silently and stare, so I asked her what she thought of Wisconsin. She told me, with an absolutely wonderful smile, that the Wisconsin countryside she had driven through looked so much like Denmark that any Dane would feel comfortable here. Then the queen, her entourage and the Secret Service were gone, speeding off into the soft spring evening.

Walking back to my car, I had another look at the little log house. It was difficult after all the glitter and ceremony to imagine what life had been like one hundred years ago in West Denmark. But surely, cut-over and stump-strewn, Polk County couldn't have reminded Pedersen of his homeland. The story of these Danish settlers is sketchy. They journeyed to Wisconsin searching for inexpensive land, to find a place where Danes of small means could establish a colony. It is known that Kristen Pedersen built this snug log house in 1872 and a few years later a two-crib log barn. It is not hard to picture him digging among the stumps of the small clearing to plant a few potatoes. And to imagine the back-breaking, agonizingly slow labor of removing rocks and stumps and trees to enlarge the clearing so that more crops might be planted. One would believe there were good times too–old country holidays to celebrate, as well as the new. One story is told of these immigrant Danes celebrating the Fourth of July with speeches and singing–while proudly flying a Danish flag.

On a recent visit to Old World Wisconsin, I walked around the Pedersen homestead, again admiring this simple, durable building with its precise inverted V-corner notching, the kitchen garden neatly spaded and ready to be planted with potatoes, kale, peas and cabbage. Just beyond stands the Jensen Barn, a two-bay log barn, its curling, silvered shingles resembling the ruffled feathers of a bird. Settled comfortably in a small clearing, lovingly preserved and brought back to life, these buildings look like home, as though they've always been here.

Living history at Old World Wisconsin, Eagle.

Patterned farmland, Bay City.

Trillium at Bass Lake Preserve, Iron County.

Early spring forest, Gordon.

Architectural contrasts, Milwaukee.

Aspen trees and red oak leaves, Gilman.

Male cardinal in a gentle snow, Hudson.

Female cardinal fluffed for warmth, Hudson.

The canoes I know and love are sleek and elegant. They glide through the water with a whisper and call up memories of clouds reflected in wilderness lakes and the haunting cry of loons. The

W H I T E W A T E R

canoe I am about to enter, to paddle down a river that obviously has too much water in it, is graceless, as stubby and wide-beamed as a sumo wrestler. It looks like it wants to pick a fight. And in George Steed it has found a perfect partner in combat.

George is a famous paddler. He not only teaches white-water canoeing and kayaking, but he teaches the teachers. He is also cocky and outspoken. Last night, while I was trying to catch a trout, he dropped by our campsite and informed my wife Nancy that he was taking me paddling on the Peshtigo the next day. There had been some rain over there and the water level was "nice." Graciously, in my absence, Nancy accepted.

Now, early the next morning, I am putting on a heavily padded helmet and thick-ribbed life vest. At the same time, I am trying not to notice the Peshtigo River, raging, running over its banks, ominously swollen by two days of heavy rain.

All around us, members of the University of Wisconsin Hoofers Outing Club are donning helmets and jackets and readying their slim kayaks. They wear warm, protective wet suits. I'm in the light rain gear I use for golf. They wear spray skirts to keep the water out of their kayaks. The canoe I'm about to ride looks like it was designed as a bathtub. They are chattering excitedly, eager to set off down the Peshtigo through Roaring Rapids, a famous, continuous, three and a half miles of awesome white water.

A few of the Hoofers stroll over and eye our open canoe skeptically. They appear to know George. With a grin and a bit of a swagger he walks past them and cups his hands around a match to light an oversized cigar.

"Ready, Howie?" he asks.

"George," says one of the Hoofers. "No one in an open canoe goes through Roaring Rapids with the water this high."

"We're going to," George replies, obviously relishing the prospect.

He steadies the canoe while I climb in and slip into the thigh straps designed to keep me in place. We push off into the roughest white water I've ever been in. The Hoofers in their kayaks flit around us like small birds harassing a crow. They are laughing. They expect to see George ejected. And, of course, when George swims, Howard swims.

At First Drop Falls we pull into shore to scout, climbing across the rocks, alongside the drop. The Hoofers' kayaks are going through, sweeping down, disappearing for a moment in the boiling water and then bobbing up. Very nicely done but an obvious portage for an open canoe, I decide.

"It's tricky," George explains, waving at the torrent, using his cigar like a baton. "What you have to watch out for is that big side curler."

"Why not portage?" I shout over the river's roar.

George shakes his head and we climb back into the squat canoe and begin paddling furiously, driving it up against the current and then spinning it downstream into the rapids. A wall of water rises up on my right, smashing into the canoe and drenching me. Miraculously we stay upright and shoot through to quieter water. "No problem," George says, puffing happily on his cigar as we paddle to shore and dump out the root beer-colored water. The Hoofers are waiting and we are on our way downstream.

Second and Third drops are brief encounters with a lot of water. But we go through them with ease and I'm beginning to feel better about the whole situation. We approach Five Foot Falls cautiously. This one we scout. We are hardly landed when two kayaks, minus their Hoofers, float by and are sucked over the falls. We leap back into our canoe to give chase. This is an absolutely irrational act because Five Foot Falls is in the way. Momentarily we hang on the lip and then the force of the water heaves us over the edge half-sideways. The canoe tips precariously and water begins to pour in. "Lean downsteam, dammit!" George yells. Sluggishly, the nearly filled canoe comes back to level and we gingerly paddle into calm water.

The Hoofers are still upstream solving their own problems and we are facing Horse Race. This is a much longer rapids, falling sharply, twisting through a narrow gorge. As I eye the portage trail, George calmly explains the complex maneuvers we are about to attempt. Then we are paddling furiously through Horse Race, a prodigious torrent of water. We skim by a jutting rock face, dive down a chute and with a great lunge ram through a massive standing wave at the bottom.

Automatically I paddle to shore, get out wearily and lift my end of the canoe to dump the water. There is no responding lift on the other end. Good lord, I think, I've lost George. But no, he's back there quietly working on his battered cigar. It emits a few wispy tendrils of smoke. He grins as we empty the canoe.

"Just S-Curve to go," he says cheerily. His cigar sends up a robust cloud of smoke. "And there's just enough of this baby left to get us through."

Mist over Big Manitou Falls, Superior.

Lightning strike at Ellsworth.

Springtime along the Chippewa River, Chippewa County.

Emerging water lily in the Mink River Estuary, Rowleys Bay.

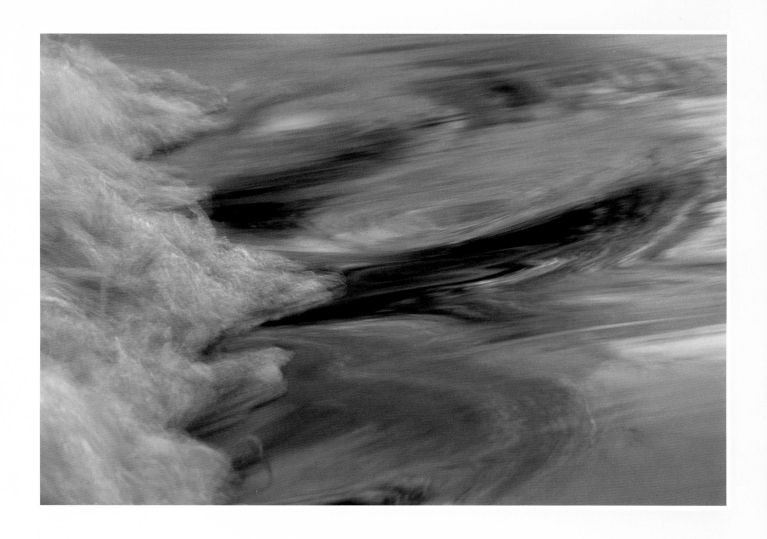

Reflections in the Wolf River, Langlade.

In the brewing tradition, Milwaukee.

Harvesting oats, Pierce County.

Night sky over Milwaukee.

Swans rising from the Black River, Onalaska.

It is a February full moon that draws us into the hills west of Madison, beyond the glare of city lights, to ski through the night. A Full Moonski–an adventure so often planned and just as often postponed. There are only

FULL MOONSKI

nine nights each year when a true Full Moonski is possible–three deep winter months multiplied by the number of nights of the true full moon and a night on either side of it. So many things can go wrong. The night is overcast, or the ground bare; too warm is just as bad as too cold. Worst of all, what if the sky is clear, the moon is full and it's a Wednesday? Can you imagine? "Dear teacher: Please excuse Andy, Becky and Jenny who missed school yesterday because they were exhausted after spending the night skiing by the light of the full moon."

But now we have snow, and plenty of it, and the day has been stunningly clear. Our plan is simple. Supper at home, a quick waxing of the skis and then the thirty-mile drive to our cabin with the full moon rising behind us. We'll haul the food, sleeping bags and dry clothes half a mile up to the cabin with the moon's brightness lighting our way.

"How's the moon?" I ask over my shoulder as we ride. "Not a cloud in sight," comes the muffled answer from kids buried under sleeping bags. When we turn off the highway and onto the road that curls through a long valley and up and over a ridge toward our place, the moon is a gleaming butter-yellow ball just clearing the hilltops. A child's voice from the rear of the wagon says in an awed tone, "Perfect."

Getting out of the warm car at the foot of the driveway, drifted solidly shut, is a shock. Moonlight gives no warmth and under the bare-boned oak branches arching over the car, it is very dark. We load the toboggan–no riders tonight–and everyone slips into their packs. The Moonski begins.

First goes the hauler of the heavily laden toboggan, on snowshoes, tromping down the fluffy snow. This bright, cold night is so quiet that we speak in whispers as we ski single file, following the luminous, frosted puffs of vapor from each breath that seem to hang motionless in the air. Across the valley on the crest of a long, smooth ridge, four deer stand watching. As we slide to a stop they turn and disappear with a bound. On again under the wintry moon, skiing to the rhythm of our breathing and the squeak of our skis in the new snow.

On a small rise stands the cabin. Surrounded by immense silver maples, it is a mysterious silhouette. We crowd inside. Now there is excited talk and laughter. Once we get a fire roaring in the Franklin stove, the oak log walls will absorb the heat and in a couple of hours the cabin will be as warm as a tropical island.

The stove loaded, gear stowed, sleeping bags laid out, we are outside again in the moonlight, heading up through the birches, following the meandering two-track road. There is hardly a level spot anywhere on our one hundred and twenty acres. It has always been a poor place to farm, but for skiing by the light of the moon, it is perfect. We have cut a web of trails everywhere, through the hills and valleys, with slopes that range from gentle to precipitous.

At the top of Dead Tree Hill, the moon is a glorious sight. High in the sky its reflected light pours down, casting sharp-edged shadows. It is so bright you could read a compass by its light if you were lost, or play Frisbee if you weren't. Ahead of us a broad, smooth field falls away to the west until it drops off into blackness. Beyond, far down the valley, are the twinkling lights of another farm.

And so we begin to ski toward these lights right to the edge of the void. Here we turn and ski down a snaky trail toward the old orchard, through wicked blackberry canes. On a sharp turn I misstep and plunge headlong into what could rightly be called a grove of them. One by one the entire family, following in my tracks, crashes until we are a tangled, laughing heap. A new leader is elected on the spot.

We ski together through the moonlight to the furthest corner of the farm and back, then herringbone to the top of the highest ridge where we can smell fragrant wood smoke and see the welcoming lights of the cabin. Then we push off, one at a time, down through the soft snow, around the bends, faster and faster to the bottom.

Hours later I get up, step carefully between the huddled forms clustered in sleeping bags around the stove and place a couple of chunks of oak on the coals. The moon is a golden globe low in the sky, hovering just above the hills. I turn away. I won't watch. As far as I'm concerned, on this one night, the moon never set.

Ice floes in Lake Michigan, Two Rivers.

Snowy owl, Mason.

Late summer harvest of gladiolas, Waushara County.

Amid shooting stars at Chiwaukee Prairie, Kenosha.

Daylight departs Maiden Rock.

Fog-shrouded fall, Winter.

Lupines and daisies, Cornucopia.

American Indian woman in traditional dress, Black River Falls.

I have always been partial to turkey vultures. One warm summer day in the Baraboo Hills I watched six or seven of these huge black birds riding the thermals, drifting up effortlessly in graceful, lazy spirals.

BIRD'S-EYE VIEW

Up close they are the ugliest birds I know, with their naked, dull red heads and necks. But in flight, swaying and tilting on immense upswept wings, they are incredibly beautiful. Thinking of them looking down on Wisconsin with those keen buzzard eyes always leaves me a bit jealous, for they enjoy the perspective I most covet–the panoramic, the lofty bird's-eye view. But, of course, these birds aren't really admiring the scenery; they are looking for their next meal. I would be satisfied with just the view.

I wouldn't say that watching turkey vultures riding the skies has ever stirred me to the point of considering flying lessons. But still, as I am more consumed with curiosity than I am by middle-aged fatalism, I have an increasing itch to get off the ground and into the sky to get a better sense of what's what. I fantasize about sweeping back and forth over the Kettle Moraine, trying to read the glacier's tracks for myself. I'd like to fly over wild, heavily wooded Forest County with a little snow on the ground, to try to figure out where I get lost every deer season and why. And I'm longing to see all the Apostle Islands, particularly those I've never gotten to sailing.

This is not to say I haven't had some unforgettable moments in the air over Wisconsin. One memorable view was squeezed through the tiny window of a jet, coming home after a long trip. Hurtling down from 30,000 feet we broke through a light gauze of clouds just over the smooth curve of Lake Michigan's shoreline. The angle of the plane was perfect to watch the sun, a splash of crimson, slide toward the horizon. The friendly southern Wisconsin farmland sketched a crazy quilt pattern–some fields partly square, others angled and pointed, and still others marvels of irregularity, held together by wood lots and the straight lines of windbreaks. Definitely land with character.

As we closed in on Madison, the countryside filled up with darkness, erasing the landmarks. Lights began to blink on in farmhouses and on the main streets of small towns. A broad sweep of Wisconsin seen in the space of a few minutes, but from the air the familiar landscape was excitingly fresh and lovely.

I've had even finer moments of flying over Wisconsin–those from a small, nimble plane, where all I had to do was reach out and touch the pilot lightly on the shoulder to get a better view. Heading north, seeing the Wisconsin River in long stretches was a startling experience. All the fragments I'd seen while paddling down on the river now came together. Highway 51 crawled with cars escaping to the north. Mostly farmland and some forest became mostly forest and lakes. As the day began to turn gray, islands became black shapes in lakes the color of gunmetal. The sun sent bright shafts of light through swelling clouds, and in the distance a single stunning lightning bolt jabbed at the earth. As we reached the airport the first drops of rain began to rattle on the wings.

Given a choice of aerial conveyance, my first by far would be a hot air balloon–the most wonderfully historic and ridiculously impractical way to fly imaginable. These colorful balloons romance the air. Their ascent is surprisingly swift and gentle. And once up, the balloon simply drifts on whatever vagrant bit of wind comes along. Except for an occasional blast from the propane burner, ballooning is remarkably quiet; conversation is easy; muted sounds rise from the world below. I can lean back against the edge of the wicker gondola with all the time in the world to enjoy the view and think soaring thoughts.

What makes ballooning even more irresistible is that it happens at my favorite times of day–early morning and evening when the air is calm. It is an ethereal view. Fields the deepest of green. Hills and ridges held apart, one from another, by deep shadows. Ground fog at dusk creeping into low places. And the soft warm light adding a rich glow to the landscape. It is this bird's-eye view of Wisconsin I carry in my heart–always changing, full of surprises, and ever so beautiful.

Wisconsin's state bird, Milwaukee County.

Under a full moon, Stevens Point.

Tulip time at the State Capitol, Madison.

On the ground at the EAA Fly-In, Oshkosh.

Birch grove in soft sunlight, Cable.